STREET GRAPHICS NEW YORK

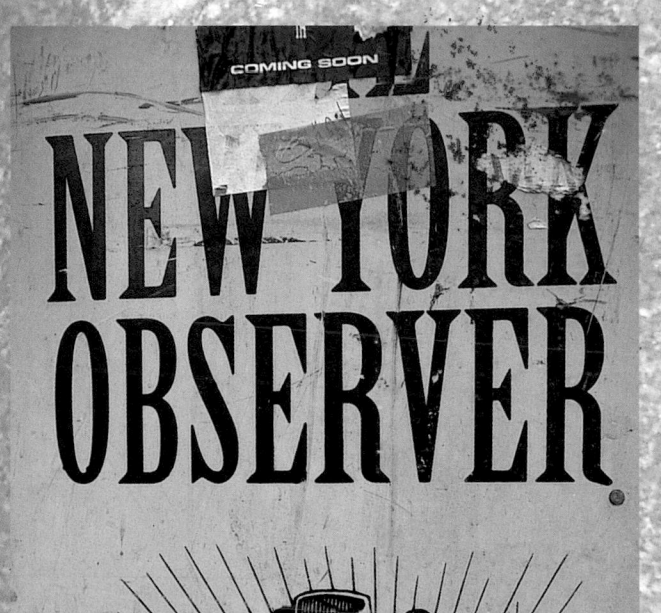

STREET
GRAPHICS
NEW YORK

BARRY DAWSON

with 208 colour illustrations

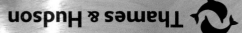 Thames & Hudson

For Sibylle – May 1, 2000, NYC

Big thanks to Rike Behrendt and Sebastian Kaufmann for making their apartment my New York home and to Eileen Connor for her hospitality and contribution ("A toast of love," p. 24). Thanks also to the following New Yorkers for their advice, hospitality, and services: Eileen Godfrey, Paula Gilhooley, Fabian Garcia and the Diapositive Bond Street Crew, Louise Hunnicut, David Bradford and his yellow cab, Avi Weiss, and Mabel Odessey for her photographic and ministerial work in NYC on May 1 2000. And, in praise of boots: The Brasher Boot Company, England – www.brasher.co.uk

Credit and thanks are due to the New York artists whose work appears here: Robert Buck and NakedCowboy.com, Federico Catteluccio, Andrew Charles, Chico, Shepard Fairey and obeygiant.com, Rico Fonseca, Hells Angels MC, Charlie Samuels, Hulbert Waldroup, Lori Leven and nyadorned.com, Matty Jankowski and SacredTattoo.com, Michelle Myles and DareDevilTattoo.com, and many more unknown.

Info: streetgraphics@fsmail.net

Any copy of this book issued by the publisher as a paperback is sold subject to the condition that it shall not by way of trade or otherwise be lent, resold, hired out or otherwise circulated without the publisher's prior consent in any form of binding or cover other than that in which it is published and without a similar condition including these words being imposed on a subsequent purchaser. First published in the United Kingdom in 2003 by Thames & Hudson Ltd, 181A High Holborn, London WC1V 7QX
www.thamesandhudson.com   © 2003 Thames & Hudson Ltd. All Rights Reserved. No part of this publication may be reproduced or transmitted in any form or by any means, electronic or mechanical, including photocopy, recording or any other information storage and retrieval system, without prior permission in writing from the publisher.
British Library Cataloguing-in-Publication Data. A catalogue record for this book is available from the British Library

ISBN 0-500-28405-9

Printed in Hong Kong by H&Y Printing Ltd

6	INTRODUCTION
12	LANDMARKS
22	MURALS
36	SIGNS, SYMBOLS & SERVICES
56	STARS & STRIPES
68	MUSIC
84	9/11
94	STENCILS & STICKERS

CONTENTS

> **The place is New York,
> the time is the present,
> and neither one will change.**
>
> Paul Auster, *The New York Tritogy*

New York is the world capital of street graphics—the urban ephemera of signs, symbols, graffiti, murals and advertising. Overlapping street graphics form a metaphor illustrating New York's dynamic sense of the present—the top layer signifies "here and now" and is in a constant state of flux. This creative edge produces innovative ideas, styles and media that are quickly copied, establishing New York's street graphics as an international benchmark.

The city's iconic landmarks, though hackneyed through representation, are continually reworked for advertising, tourist souvenirs and, in the wake of the events of September 11, 2001, for patriotic propaganda. The World Trade Center attack and its aftermath unfolded like a storyboard across the walls and sidewalks of New York City. Expressions of shock, outrage and grief were stenciled, painted and written, along with accolades for heroism, demands for reprisal and pleas for peace. Then New York and its street graphics moved on—reactionary statements were replaced with imagery of resilience and humor, hallmarks of New York City.

INTRODUCTION

> ## What is barely hinted in other American cities is condensed and enlarged in New York.
>
> Saul Bellow

The island borough of Manhattan measures only 23 square miles, but the small but dense urban grid formed by its intersecting streets and avenues is a vast canvas for artistic expression, rich in its range and scale. To observe the streets of New York requires both an eye for detail and an overview. A sticker the size of a postage stamp can detract from a nearby mural covering several stories of a building, or perhaps a stenciled image underfoot. Competition is fierce at eye level, thick layers of ephemera coat the streetlights, and posters are plastered onto abandoned buildings and construction site fences.

Above and below eye level, the city's past peers through the here and now—nostalgic graffiti on the basement wall of a defunct 1960s music venue, a fading fallout shelter sign (a forgotten relic of the Cold War) high above a school doorway, or a corporate logo standing the test of time to become a familiar landmark. The intensity of Manhattan's street graphics command attention, with an energy that sometimes spills into Brooklyn and the other outer boroughs of New York City.

INTRODUCTION

> In 1919,
> with the permission
> and with the approval
> of other Dadaists,
> I legalized Dada in New York.

Man Ray, "Who Made Dada?"

Street art has a reputable history in New York. "Found" imagery was incorporated into the work of Man Ray, who was brought up in the city and became a leading figure in the prewar Dada and Surrealist art movements. Lifelong Queens resident and artist Joseph Cornell scoured the city for ephemera to be used in his "shadow boxes." Photographer Walker Evans documented and collected the city's signs for over forty years. New York artists Robert Rauschenberg and Jasper Johns used street motifs in their seminal 1950s work. Icons of popular culture were central for Andy Warhol and the New York Pop Art movement of the 1960s. Today's hip-hop artwork has its roots in New York's cryptic graffiti style of "tagging," developed in the Bronx during the 1970s. Artist Keith Haring risked arrest drawing in the city's subways in the 1980s; his work then transferred to galleries and remains internationally popular on merchandise. Since its legalization in 1997, tattooing has become a popular medium of visual expression in the city. New York's current "outlaw" media are stencils and stickers: fast to execute, easy to repeat and infinitely replaceable.

This book is a subjective glimpse at the city's street graphics from April 2000 to September 2002.

INTRODUCTION

New York buildings?
They aren't modest buildings,
plain residential complexes.
No, they are statements.

David Bradford, *Drive-By Shootings*

LANDMARKS

The Statue of Liberty represented in a commercial fashion house mural, a landmark in its own right, on East Houston Street.

14 The Statue of Liberty represented on a 1940s needlebook, a contemporary Brooklyn mural, a souvenir tie, a phonecard, and a 1950s souvenir cushion cover. Originally designed as a lighthouse for the Suez Canal titled "Egypt Carrying the Light to Asia," the statue was rejected, remodeled and renamed "Liberty Enlightening the World." Unveiled in New York harbor in 1886, it has become an international icon of freedom.

Souvenir of

NEW YORK

United Nations Building

Empire State Building

RCA Building Radio City

16   42nd Street: the bronze Art Deco facade of the 1929 Chanin Building. 34th Street: Macy's department store sign derives its star logo from a tattoo on the arm of its founder (and former whaler) Rowland Hussey Macy. An inflatable representation of fictional Queens resident Spider-Man, crawling down the Loews Theater facade for the local premiere of *Spider-Man* the movie. The Guggenheim Museum, architect Frank Lloyd Wright's controversial 1959 masterpiece.

Broadway's 1913 Woolworth Building depicted on a 1940s needlebook in a NY flea market, a neon sign in Greenwich Village's Christopher Street, and representations of New York's classic Art Deco skyscrapers: the 1930 Chrysler Building on a bronze Park Avenue plaque and the 1931 Empire State Building on a Midtown neon deli sign.
Overleaf: Central Park cycle path and Brooklyn Bridge footpath symbols.

Below, the Chelsea Hotel on 23rd Street. Notable residents have included Mark Twain, Sarah Bernhardt, Dylan Thomas, Jasper Johns, William S. Burroughs, Bob Dylan and Sid Vicious. Opposite, New York hotels depicted on a collection of 1940s matchbooks in a Chelsea flea market.

RETURN your mind to its upright position.

Painting relates to both art and life.

Robert Rauschenberg

MURALS

A commercial mural for Amtrak, opposite the New Yorker Hotel on 34th Street.

Advertising murals on Houston Street and community murals in the East Village and Spanish Harlem.

Mural details in New York's lively East Village featuring images of death, mutation and pestilence.
Overleaf: An East Village mural depicting metamorphosis.

30 Details of monochrome murals in the Bowery, St. Mark's Place, 23rd Street, Williamsburg, and the East Village.
Overleaf: Wall mural outside the Veselka Ukrainian restaurant on Second Avenue.

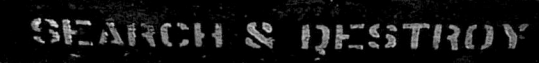

A mural on Avenue C reading "Loisaida," the Hispanic phonetic spelling of "Lower East Side."

Women represented as spray-painted male fantasies adorn walls and doors in Brooklyn and Midtown. Below, life imitates art beside a Bowery garage mural.

**Word begets image
and image *is* virus.**

William S. Burroughs

SIGNS, SYMBOLS & SERVICES

Window detail of the Greenwich Village
tattoo and body-piercing store Village Pop.

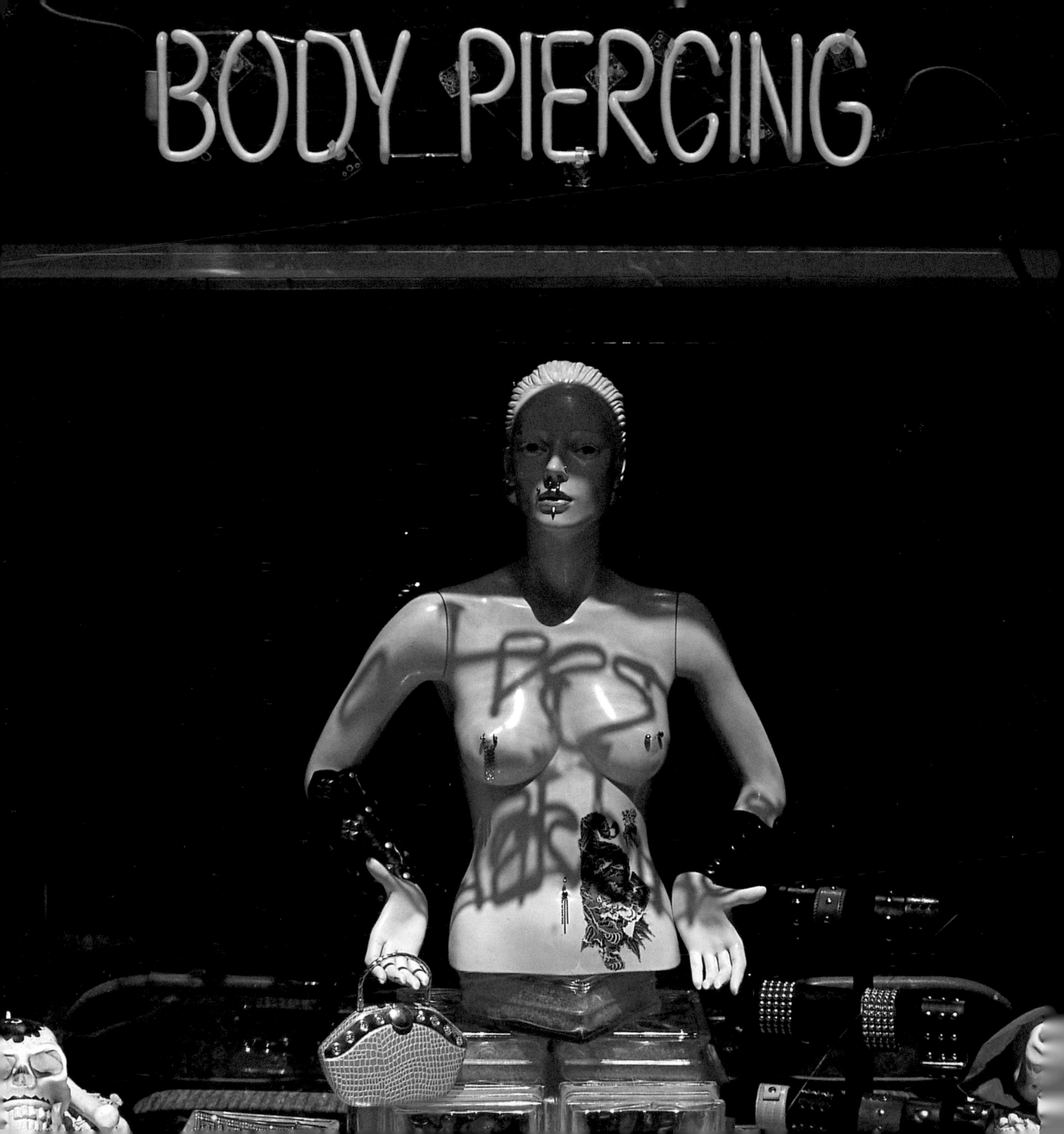

Body-art store-window detail in Greenwich Village. Hand tattoos by Michelle Myles of Dare Devil Tattoo, arm tattoos by New York Adorned and Sacred Tattoo, and a shoulder tattoo from Bowery Tattoo.
Overleaf: New York's coolest are tattooed by New York Adorned (left) and Sacred Tattoo (center and right). Outlawed by the NYC Health Department from 1962 until 1997, tattooing is undergoing a renaissance.

44   *Previous pages:* The winged horse sign of Mobil Gas outside an East Houston Street antique store. Andy Warhol had one on his 1960s New York apartment wall.
These pages: The ubiquitous neon signs of Times Square and side streets of lower Manhattan.

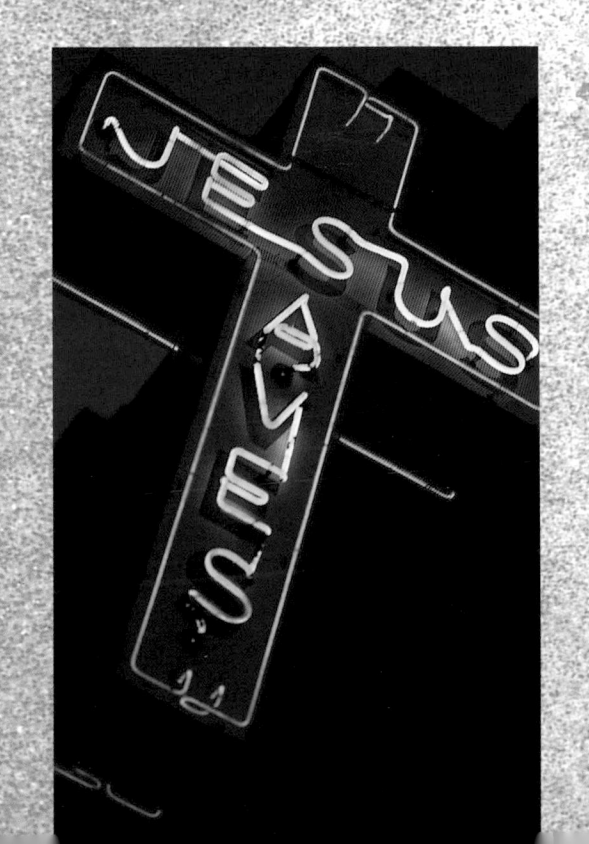

Neon signs in the windows of a Manhattan nail parlor and astrologist. Opposite, the arguably perfect physique represented on an East Village gym sign invites the addition of a humorous speech bubble sticker.

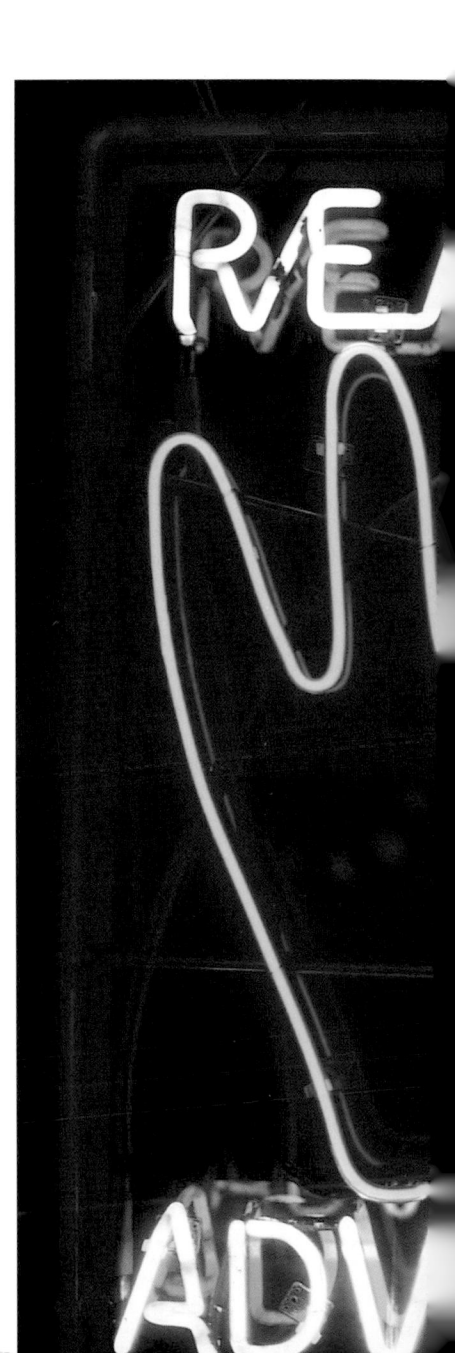

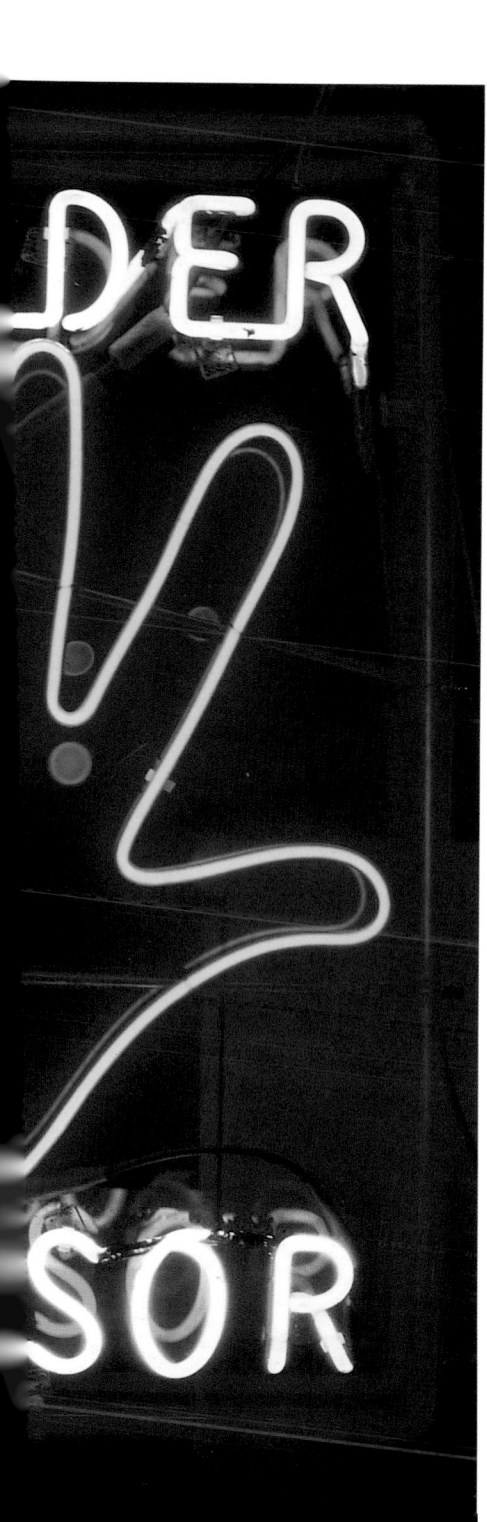

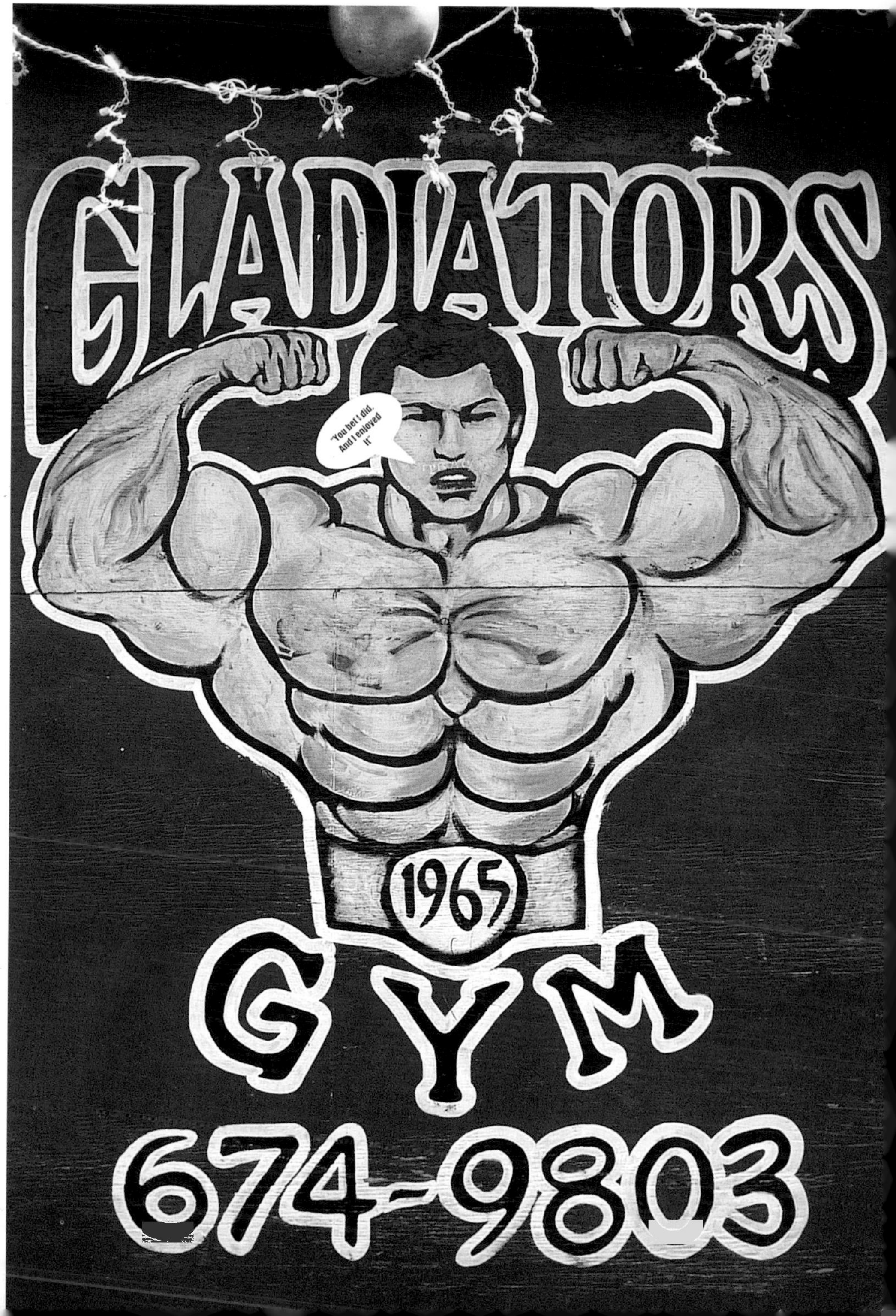

CAPACITY

FALLOUT SHELTER
IN BASEMENT

Previous pages: Architectural detail of a 23rd Street school building with a 1960s nuclear fallout shelter sign.
These pages: Humorous hand-rendered signs, East Village. A sticker-covered door welcomes patrons to the friendly
Hogs & Heifers saloon in Manhattan's West Side meatpacking district.

IN MEMORY OF

LT Billy McGinn

FF Eric Allen   FF Andy Fredericks

FF Dave Halderman   FF Timmy Haskell

FF Manny Mojica   FF Larry Virgilio

WE WILL NEVER FORGET

1976

Previous pages: America's independence bicentennial is celebrated on a FDNY station door mural in Greenwich Village. *These pages:* Registration number stenciled on a yellow taxi door; a defunct checkered cab represented in an East Village mosaic, and a wheel arch detail of an original model; Pop artist Roy Lichtenstein's futuristic train mural in Times Square subway station and a defaced NYPD slogan and badge stencil in Brooklyn.

New Yorkers are probably more patriotic than they've been in a long time.

Rudolph Giuliani

A tow truck covered in flags.

STARS & STRIPES

Top row: A Staten Island diner painted in stars & stripes, a patriotic clothing-store window display in Manhattan, and a truck airbrushed in patriotic livery with national landmarks featured in the letterforms.

Bottom row: A painted flag and slogan in a store window, detail of a patriotic paint job on a Vietnam War veteran's Harley-Davidson motorcycle, and another clothing-store window-display detail.

59

The Naked Cowboy,
a Times Square street
performer, with patriotic
colors on his guitar.

Ties on sale at Rockefeller Center, a Midtown hat-store display, and a needlepoint cushion in a store window.

Previous pages: Detail of a Coney Island amusement arcade machine filled with inflatable patriotic prizes.
These pages: Stars & stripes bedroom slippers at a Chelsea flea market, featuring caricatures of former US President Ronald Reagan and First Lady Nancy. Below, a sticker and stencil in Manhattan featuring stars & stripes.

Contemporary posters promoting music in Manhattan and Brooklyn.
Overleaf: A poster promoting the rock band Supergarage in the window of famous Bleecker Street club The Bitter End.

spinnilicious! Hellon Wheels

8/24 SATURDAY

spinnilicious!

special guests:
Tom Stabb
DJ Muscles

Southside Lounge
41 Bway bet. Wythe & Ker

Spinnilicious! is the After-Party for the opening of "On The Waterfront" at Open Ground Gallery, 252 Grand Street, Reception 8-12

The intimation of mortality
is part of New York now;
in the sounds of jets overhead,
in the black headlines
of the latest editions.

E. B. White, *Here is New York*, 1949

A commemorative mural in the East Village, illustrating
the WTC twin towers moments after the impact by
terrorist-hijacked planes.

9/11

Opposite, a Midtown flag mural, with the stars representing America's states replaced with a stylized representation of the WTC towers. Below, a flag at Ground Zero and a mural in Queens depict the US national bird, a Bald Eagle; a flag draped over a Coney Island truck; hard hats and flag at the Ground Zero Memorial.

88   "A toast of love"—skywriting above the WTC's twin towers marks a wedding celebration in "Windows on the World," a restaurant on the 107th floor, 1986. Below, the towers represented on memorial murals in the East Village and Williamsburg, and on a FDNY commemorative T-shirt.

Posters at the Ground Zero Memorial, a Brooklyn mural and resin figures at a Chelsea flea market signify the loss of life in New York's public services on September 11, 2001.
Overleaf: Detail of a Greenwich Village ceramic tile memorial.

Details from a T-shirt, a stenciled epitaph in Union Square, an "abridged" *New York Post* front page, and street drawings illustrate a call for retribution. Below, a Harlem mural marks the city's grief with a depiction of the Statue of Liberty crying blood.

Peace and freedom, represented by the white dove and Liberty's torch, signify resilience and rebirth in this East Village mural detail of the Statue of Liberty emerging from the WTC ruins. Center, a bold graphic sticker urges New Yorkers to remember the WTC tragedy. Opposite, two banks of searchlights, installed at Ground Zero and viewed from the Empire State Building, simulate the twin towers and mark the six-month anniversary of 9/11.

I love an image
that is worth repeating.

Andy Warhol

"Obey Giant" stencil and sticker images by artist
Shepard Fairey. The original stencil appeared in 1989;
based on an image of a 7'4" Russian wrestler, it was
captioned "Andre the Giant has a Posse," satirizing
cliquey skateboard gangs. Shepard Fairey developed
the image into a campaign challenging public
perceptions of advertising.

STENCILS & STICKERS

Stencil and spray-paint statements on the walls and sidewalks of Manhattan.
Overleaf: A typical New York City sign, almost obliterated with sticker images.

Stenciled images in Soho and the East Village
Overleaf: Ephemera decorating the doorway of Marty's Cool Stuff antique store on Lafayette Street.

101

Stickers on the walls of Tribeca and the East Village, and a Williamsburg door featuring both stencil and sticker imagery.

DEATH NURSE 2000

Lady trouble

© 2002 cm / zimbo

benfRank

Remnants of a rain-soaked poster in Manhattan, and a spray-painted stencil.
Overleaf: A simple pig stencil creates a strong image on the crumbling paint of an East Village wall.

Stenciled statements satirizing the propaganda of patriotism, and a stenciled NYPD barrier. *Overleaf:* The New York plastic bag. The original "I Love NY" logo was the response of noted graphic designer Milton Glaser to a commission to create a new image for the tarnished New York of 1976.

New York is an ugly city, a dirty city.
Its climate is a scandal, its politics are
used to frighten children, its traffic is
madness, its competition is murderous.
But there is one thing about it—once you
have lived in New York and it has become
your home, no place else is good enough.

John Steinbeck, "The Making of a New Yorker"